OPERATOR AI
Artificial Intelligence That Can Do More Than Chat

Exploring OpenAI's Breakthrough Technology and What It Means for Every Industry

J. Andy Peters

Copyright ©J. Andy Peters, *2024.*

All rights reserved. No part of this publication may be reproduced, distributed, or transmitted in any form or by any means, including photocopying, recording, or other electronic or mechanical methods, without the prior written permission of the publisher, except in the case of brief quotations embodied in critical reviews and certain other noncommercial uses permitted by copyright law.

Table of Contents

Introduction: The Era of AI Agents.............................. 3
Chapter 1: What is Operator AI?................................. 6
The Role of Probabilistic Decision-Making.............. 12
How It Manages Tasks... 13
Multi-Tasking Across the Web..................................15
The Technology Behind the Adaptability................. 16
Chapter 2: The Rise of Autonomous AI.................... 19
Chapter 3: The Technology Behind Operator.......... 30
Chapter 4: Practical Applications of Operator.........45
Chapter 5: The Future of Work in the Age of AI Agents... 62
Chapter 6: Ethical Considerations of Autonomous AI 76
Chapter 7: The Business Implications of Operator. 91
Chapter 8: The Environmental Impact of AI........... 113
Chapter 9: Accessibility and the Democratization of AI.. 124
Chapter 10: What's Next for AI Agents?.................136
Conclusion... 152

Introduction: The Era of AI Agents

Artificial intelligence has come a long way in the past few decades. From the early days of simple chatbots answering basic questions to more sophisticated systems capable of processing vast amounts of data, AI has continuously pushed the boundaries of what machines can do. Yet, for all its advancements, most AI systems still relied on human direction, performing tasks only within predefined limits. That all started to change with the development of AI agents. These agents, unlike traditional chatbots, are designed to think independently, learn from their environment, and make decisions that go beyond simple queries. They take on multi-step tasks and execute actions autonomously, making them far more versatile and powerful than anything we've seen before.

OpenAI's "Operator" represents a leap forward in this new wave of AI technology. While typical AI systems might provide responses to your questions or help you navigate through simple tasks, Operator does much more. It can book travel, manage workflows, process complex data, and even make real-time decisions based on the context. The key difference is that Operator is built to handle entire processes from start to finish, without constant prompts or human intervention. This shift is revolutionary because it moves AI from a tool that simply assists to one that actively carries out real tasks across various platforms and industries. Operator's ability to adapt, learn, and evolve in real-time makes it more like a digital assistant you can truly rely on.

The purpose of this book is to explore this new chapter in AI's evolution. We'll look closely at OpenAI's Operator, delving into its capabilities, the technology behind it, and its potential impact on various sectors—from customer service to healthcare to everyday tasks. This book will help readers understand how AI agents like Operator can reshape industries, transform work processes, and influence daily life. We'll also explore the challenges, ethical considerations, and future implications as AI agents become an integral part of our digital landscape.

Chapter 1: What is Operator AI?

AI agents represent a fundamentally different class of artificial intelligence compared to the chatbots many of us are familiar with. While both are powered by AI, the key difference lies in their capabilities and the way they interact with users and systems. Chatbots, at their core, are designed to respond to specific queries and engage in conversation. They work by following programmed instructions or pre-defined rules, processing one step at a time, and often require ongoing input from the user to guide the conversation. Essentially, chatbots are great for answering questions or handling simple tasks, but they are limited to a reactive role, always waiting for a prompt before they act.

AI agents, on the other hand, are far more sophisticated and autonomous. They are designed not only to respond to requests but also to take action independently, completing entire processes or workflows without needing constant human input. Imagine an AI that can schedule your meetings, book your travel, organize a complex project, or manage your email inbox—all by itself. These agents are built to make decisions, adapt to changing circumstances, and carry out tasks with little to no intervention from the user. Unlike chatbots, which simply follow pre-set paths, AI agents are dynamic. They can think on their feet, adjust their actions based on new information, and even pivot when something unexpected happens, just like a human assistant would.

Take, for example, OpenAI's Operator. This AI agent is designed to move between multiple tasks, from searching for flights to processing transactions, all with minimal input from the user. You could tell it the type of flight you're looking for, and it would handle everything from finding options to booking the ticket—adjusting its approach along the way if needed. The ability of AI agents to tackle multi-step tasks and execute decisions independently marks a significant leap forward in the AI field. These systems aren't just reactive, they are proactive, making them capable of handling more complex responsibilities that were once solely in the hands of humans.

In this new era, AI agents are set to revolutionize how we interact with technology, making them not just tools, but valuable collaborators capable of seamlessly integrating into our workflows and daily lives. As this technology evolves, AI agents will likely become indispensable, not just for businesses but for individuals as well, acting as personal assistants, task managers, and decision-making partners.

Operator is a game-changing AI agent, designed with a set of key features that make it stand out from its predecessors. What sets it apart is its ability to work directly within web browsers, allowing it to seamlessly interact with multiple websites, tabs, and applications, much like a human assistant navigating through digital tasks. This feature is fundamental to its design, as it enables

Operator to take over processes that typically require constant user input, eliminating the need for manual work in a way that is both efficient and effective.

One of the most remarkable abilities of Operator is its capacity to automate a variety of tasks. From booking flights to coding, managing workflows, and even organizing complex schedules, Operator can handle multiple steps of a process autonomously. This makes it much more than a tool for answering questions. Imagine, for example, needing to plan a trip: instead of browsing several sites for flight options, comparing prices, and making decisions about the best times to fly, you could simply instruct Operator on your preferences, and it would take care of the rest. It could find flights, filter them based on your criteria, select the best one, and even finalize the purchase, all without requiring any further input. This level of automation frees up time and reduces the complexity of tasks that were once time-consuming and repetitive.

The true brilliance of Operator lies in its adaptability. Unlike basic automation systems, which rely on rigid rules and instructions, Operator uses a process known as probabilistic decision-making. This means it can adjust its actions in real-time based on what it encounters during the task. If it faces an obstacle—whether it's a website that doesn't load properly or an unexpected piece of data—it doesn't simply stop. Instead, it recalculates and adapts its approach, adjusting its course of action to continue moving forward. This feature makes Operator more like a human assistant than a traditional AI. It has the ability to learn from its environment, adapt to new situations, and make small decisions along the way to ensure tasks are completed effectively and efficiently.

In essence, Operator combines the best of both worlds: the precision and reliability of automation with the flexibility and problem-solving skills typically associated with human intelligence. This breakthrough technology is designed to simplify complex processes, allowing it to handle multiple tasks that were previously impossible for AI to manage on its own. It's a powerful tool that offers a glimpse into the future of AI—one where agents work independently, making decisions and carrying out tasks in real-time, with minimal input from humans.

To understand how Operator works, we need to dive into the technology that powers it and how it enables the system to function so seamlessly across a variety of tasks. At the core of Operator's functionality is a principle known as **probabilistic decision-making**, which differentiates it from earlier AI systems and traditional automation tools. This principle allows Operator to make real-time adjustments, enabling it to tackle complex tasks with greater flexibility and autonomy than previous AI models.

The Role of Probabilistic Decision-Making

Probabilistic decision-making refers to a method of processing information where the AI doesn't follow rigid, pre-programmed rules. Instead, it evaluates the available data and makes decisions based on probabilities, assessing the likelihood of certain outcomes. This ability to calculate multiple possible solutions, adjusting to changing conditions as it proceeds, is a key feature that makes Operator much more versatile and capable than other AI tools.

For example, when tasked with booking a flight, Operator doesn't just follow a list of instructions, like "go to the flight booking site, search for flights, and select the cheapest one." Instead, it processes various factors in real time, such as available flight options, user preferences (like preferred airlines, travel dates, etc.), and other dynamic elements (like changing prices or availability). If a flight option that fits the user's needs becomes unavailable or if a better option is found after the initial search, Operator is able to adjust its approach based on the new information, ensuring the best outcome.

This adaptability is a hallmark of **machine learning** and **artificial intelligence**. As Operator encounters new situations, it continuously evaluates its options, learning from prior actions to improve its decision-making over time. This makes it far more reliable and human-like in its approach, able to respond to unexpected variables and solve problems that might otherwise require human intervention.

How It Manages Tasks

The process starts when a user provides Operator with a set of instructions. These instructions are typically more general and flexible than the rigid, step-by-step commands used in traditional automation. For example, you might ask Operator to "book a flight for me to New York next week." Operator will break down that request into multiple steps—searching for available flights, comparing prices, filtering options based on preferences (e.g., best times to travel), and then booking the flight. During this process, Operator constantly monitors the situation and makes decisions at each step, ensuring that the best possible choices are made at every juncture.

Operator's real-time adaptability also comes into play when it encounters challenges. Suppose a website where the flight data is hosted fails to load properly. Unlike a traditional bot, which would simply stop and throw an error, Operator can decide to search for an alternative site or adjust its current course to bypass the problem. If, for example, a user's chosen flight is suddenly overbooked, Operator can automatically re-search for new flight options and present the best alternatives—without requiring the user to intervene.

This autonomous decision-making process is powered by a combination of advanced **natural**

language processing (NLP) algorithms and machine learning models that enable the AI to understand context and intent in the user's instructions. This allows Operator to carry out tasks that would require a human assistant to manage, as it possesses not only the capability to carry out specific actions but also the judgment to adjust to real-time events and make decisions accordingly.

Multi-Tasking Across the Web

One of the most impressive aspects of Operator is its ability to interact with multiple web pages, tabs, and applications simultaneously, effectively managing complex workflows. For example, if tasked with booking a flight, Operator might need to open several tabs—one for comparing flight prices, another for looking at accommodation options, and yet another for transportation. As it works through these tasks, Operator can simultaneously make decisions in one window based on what it finds in another, adjusting its actions without needing constant input from the user.

This capacity to move across digital environments, while continuously adapting to new information, is what allows Operator to automate tasks that would typically require significant time and effort. Whether it's making bookings, coding, managing emails, or handling customer service inquiries, Operator's seamless integration with the web and its ability to make context-aware adjustments make it a powerful, autonomous tool that could transform a wide range of industries.

The Technology Behind the Adaptability

Operator's adaptability is powered by several core technologies:

1. **Machine Learning**: Operator's algorithms learn from every task it executes. As it processes data and interacts with different systems, it continuously refines its decision-making

process, improving its ability to predict outcomes and adapt its behavior accordingly.

2. **Natural Language Processing (NLP)**: NLP allows Operator to understand and process human language, enabling it to comprehend user instructions even when phrased loosely or ambiguously. This is key to its ability to perform tasks without requiring overly specific commands.

3. **Multi-Agent Systems**: Operator's design allows it to communicate and interact with multiple systems at once, a necessity when carrying out complex tasks. The multi-agent framework ensures that different parts of a task can be executed in parallel, improving efficiency and speed.

4. **Cloud Computing**: Because Operator operates in a web browser, it relies on cloud-based infrastructure to handle the massive computing power required for processing and adapting to real-time changes. Cloud computing ensures that Operator can scale its capabilities, handling

large and complex tasks quickly without overloading local devices.

The combination of these technologies allows Operator to function not only as an assistant but as an intelligent agent capable of executing tasks in a manner similar to a human. It can process information, learn from experiences, and adjust its strategies to ensure tasks are completed successfully—making it a powerful tool in a range of industries.

Chapter 2: The Rise of Autonomous AI

AI has come a long way from its early days, when it was limited to static, rule-based models that followed rigid instructions with little room for flexibility or adaptability. In the past, AI systems were essentially confined to pre-programmed tasks, unable to learn or adjust based on the circumstances they encountered. They functioned on a simple if-then logic, following a fixed set of rules to process inputs and produce outputs. While these early models were a step forward in technology, they lacked the ability to handle the complex, real-world scenarios that businesses and individuals face every day.

Fast forward to today, and we see AI undergoing a radical transformation. The rise of dynamic AI agents, such as OpenAI's Operator, marks a significant departure from the limitations of static models. These new agents are designed to perform multi-step tasks autonomously, adapting to changes and making decisions based on real-time information. Rather than simply responding to isolated prompts, they can manage workflows, solve problems, and even take initiative in ways that were previously unimaginable.

This shift is largely driven by advances in machine learning, particularly in areas like probabilistic decision-making. These dynamic agents do not just follow a fixed set of instructions. Instead, they assess the situation, weigh different outcomes, and adjust their actions accordingly. They have the ability to learn from experience, making small decisions along the way that help them achieve their end goals. This means that unlike static models, dynamic agents can think on their feet, respond to unexpected changes, and continuously improve their performance as they interact with the world.

One of the most significant advantages of this shift is the agent's ability to perform tasks that require multiple steps, which would have been difficult for traditional AI systems to handle. For example, a static model might be able to give you a list of flight options when you're planning a trip, but it would stop there. You'd still need to manually compare options, make decisions, and complete the booking. In contrast, an AI agent like Operator can manage the entire process, from finding the best flight to purchasing the ticket, all without needing human input at each step. This level of autonomy marks a true evolution in the way AI interacts with the world.

As this transition from static models to dynamic agents continues, it's clear that AI is no longer just a tool that reacts to commands—it's becoming a true assistant capable of taking on a variety of tasks across industries. Whether it's helping businesses streamline operations, assisting in personal productivity, or even managing complex systems in real-time, the potential for these agents is immense. The era of static, rule-based AI is giving way to a new generation of agents that are not only smarter but also more capable of handling the complexities of our increasingly dynamic world.

OpenAI's vision for agent-based AI represents a bold step forward in the evolution of artificial intelligence. For years, AI models like chatbots have been powerful tools, capable of answering questions and generating responses. However, OpenAI recognized that in order to unlock the true potential of AI, these models needed to evolve beyond passive, reactive systems into dynamic, autonomous agents that could take on more complex, real-world tasks.

The motivation behind creating Operator stems from this very idea: to move AI from being a tool that simply responds to commands, into a more proactive, independent system that can manage intricate workflows, make decisions on the fly, and adapt to changing circumstances. Operator isn't just a chatbot that answers questions—it's an intelligent agent capable of completing multi-step tasks that require judgment, adaptability, and real-time decision-making. This shift towards agent-based AI is driven by OpenAI's recognition that, to remain relevant in an increasingly automated world, AI needs to be more than a simple conversational tool. It needs to become a fully capable assistant that can take on significant, high-value responsibilities across industries.

OpenAI's belief in the future of AI agents is rooted in a fundamental change in how businesses and individuals approach productivity. With AI becoming more integrated into every aspect of our lives, from customer service to healthcare to personal organization, the demand for intelligent systems that can handle more than simple queries is growing rapidly. OpenAI sees agent-based AI as the next logical step in this progression, providing a framework for systems that can autonomously tackle tasks like scheduling, managing workflows, booking services, and even coding, all with minimal human intervention.

At the heart of this vision is the belief that AI agents will ultimately revolutionize how we interact with technology. Rather than requiring constant inputs and oversight, agents like Operator are designed to function independently, adjusting their actions based on real-time data and feedback. This evolution aligns with OpenAI's larger mission to build AI that is not just intelligent but also practical and applicable in real-world scenarios.

The company believes that the future of AI lies in creating agents capable of handling complex tasks with a level of autonomy that frees up human time and energy for more strategic, high-level thinking. Instead of merely automating repetitive tasks, AI agents have the potential to take over the decision-making process entirely in some cases, helping users navigate complex challenges more effectively and efficiently.

In many ways, OpenAI sees the development of agents like Operator as an essential part of a larger trend in the AI industry. As other companies like

Microsoft, Google, and Anthropic race to build their own autonomous AI systems, the shift from rule-based, static AI to intelligent agents that can operate autonomously is becoming a central focus. OpenAI's investment in this technology, particularly through tools like Operator, reflects the company's commitment to staying at the forefront of AI innovation and to pushing the boundaries of what artificial intelligence can achieve.

Ultimately, OpenAI envisions a future where AI agents like Operator are seamlessly integrated into daily life, working alongside humans to handle tasks, solve problems, and drive productivity. Whether in the workplace, at home, or in industries across the globe, these agents have the potential to reshape how we interact with technology, enabling a more efficient, autonomous world.

The race to develop autonomous AI agents is heating up, with OpenAI at the forefront but facing strong competition from other key players in the field. Companies like Anthropic and Microsoft are making significant strides in the AI agent space, each with their own vision of what the future of artificial intelligence should look like. While OpenAI's Operator is one of the most advanced and widely recognized autonomous agents, it's not alone in this rapidly evolving landscape. The race to create AI systems that can function autonomously and handle real-world tasks is becoming a critical point of focus for these companies, as they recognize the transformative potential of such technology.

Anthropic, a newer player in the AI market, is making waves with its approach to AI development, particularly in the area of safety and transparency. Their contributions to autonomous AI are rooted in a deep focus on creating systems that are not only capable of performing complex tasks but also aligned with human values and ethical guidelines. Anthropic's flagship models, like Claude, are designed to be more adaptable and explainable, addressing concerns about the potential risks and ethical implications of increasingly autonomous AI systems. While OpenAI has been more focused on scaling its models to tackle real-world tasks, Anthropic's primary concern lies in ensuring these systems are safe, transparent, and accountable, without compromising on performance.

Microsoft, on the other hand, has been investing heavily in AI research and development, particularly through its partnership with OpenAI. While Microsoft is known for its broad range of technologies, from software like Windows and Azure to its growing presence in AI with tools like Copilot, it is making notable progress in the AI agent space as well. Their investment in OpenAI is central to their strategy of integrating advanced AI into products like Microsoft 365, where autonomous agents are increasingly being used to automate workflows, enhance productivity, and assist users with tasks ranging from scheduling to content creation. Microsoft's contribution to the autonomous AI race lies in its ability to seamlessly integrate these intelligent systems into existing ecosystems, making them more accessible to businesses and consumers alike.

The competition between OpenAI, Anthropic, and Microsoft is not just about who can build the most advanced AI agents but also about how these systems will be deployed and integrated into everyday life. While OpenAI is pushing the boundaries of what AI agents like Operator can do, Anthropic is focused on ensuring that these advancements are safe and ethically sound. Microsoft, with its vast resources and enterprise focus, is prioritizing the scalability and integration of AI agents into real-world business environments.

Despite their different approaches, these companies share a common vision: a future where autonomous AI agents are essential tools that handle more complex tasks, assist with decision-making, and integrate seamlessly into both personal and professional life. The competition is fierce, but each company's contributions are helping to shape the direction of AI development, ensuring that the future of intelligent agents is both innovative and responsible.

As the race continues, the real question is not just which company will create the most powerful AI agent, but which will successfully navigate the challenges of safety, usability, and integration. OpenAI, Anthropic, and Microsoft are all working toward the same end goal: to create AI systems that can handle real-world tasks with a level of autonomy and intelligence that can reshape industries and redefine how humans interact with technology. The journey is far from over, but the pace of innovation in autonomous AI is accelerating, and the competition is only just beginning.

Chapter 3: The Technology Behind Operator

Probabilistic decision-making is a fundamental concept that enables autonomous AI agents to navigate the complexities and uncertainties of the real world. Unlike traditional rule-based systems that rely on fixed instructions, probabilistic decision-making allows AI agents to make decisions based on likelihoods and patterns rather than certainties. This approach mirrors how humans make decisions in uncertain environments—often relying on probabilities, past experiences, and contextual clues to guide actions.

In the context of AI agents like OpenAI's Operator, probabilistic decision-making is crucial for handling real-world tasks that are dynamic and unpredictable. For example, when an AI agent is tasked with scheduling a meeting, it doesn't just follow rigid rules about availability and preferences; it considers the likelihood of conflicting schedules, the preferences of different participants, and even the potential for future changes. If a meeting is already scheduled and one participant suddenly becomes unavailable, the AI agent can assess the probability of rescheduling options and select the best course of action, adjusting as new information becomes available.

What sets probabilistic decision-making apart from traditional deterministic methods is its ability to adapt. While deterministic systems follow set rules and paths, probabilistic models constantly adjust based on new data, learning from their environment and the outcomes of their previous decisions. For example, if an AI agent encounters a new situation it hasn't been explicitly programmed to handle, it can assess the possible outcomes based on probability, weighing the most likely options and testing them against real-world feedback. Over time, this enables the agent to improve its decision-making process and adapt to new, unseen scenarios.

This adaptability is especially important when the tasks at hand are multifaceted or require ongoing adjustments. In many industries, tasks are not as simple as completing a series of predefined steps. They often require judgment, trade-offs, and decisions in the face of conflicting information. Whether it's in healthcare, where an AI might need to prioritize patient treatments based on changing conditions, or in business, where scheduling software needs to account for multiple time zones and meeting priorities, probabilistic decision-making allows the AI to navigate these complexities with greater efficiency.

Furthermore, this method of decision-making is essential for AI systems that aim to perform multiple steps or interact with other systems and users. For instance, when Operator is tasked with managing workflows, it needs to predict the outcomes of various actions and adjust its approach accordingly. If a task is delayed, the agent must assess the likelihood of it affecting other tasks, adjust schedules, or even find alternative ways to achieve the desired outcome. This constant recalibration based on probabilities is what makes AI agents so powerful—they are not static or bound by fixed rules but instead operate within a framework that allows them to think on their feet and make decisions that evolve over time.

In addition to increasing efficiency, probabilistic decision-making also plays a significant role in reducing human error. By relying on data-driven insights and statistical models, AI agents can make more informed decisions than a human might be able to in the same scenario. This doesn't mean AI replaces human judgment, but rather that it enhances it, offering insights and recommendations that consider all the possible variables that might influence an outcome. Over time, as the AI agent collects more data, its probabilistic models become more accurate, refining its predictions and improving its ability to make decisions in real-time.

The importance of probabilistic decision-making for autonomous AI agents lies in its ability to transform abstract data into actionable insights that can be applied to a wide range of tasks. Whether it's automating administrative functions, managing logistics, or making personalized recommendations, AI agents equipped with probabilistic decision-making can perform at a level that not only meets but often exceeds traditional automation capabilities. This capacity to handle real-world complexity and uncertainty is what will ultimately define the success of autonomous AI systems like OpenAI's Operator in industries across the globe.

Operator's ability to adapt in the face of unexpected challenges is what truly sets it apart from earlier AI models and chatbots. The world is full of complexities, surprises, and variables that static systems can't easily handle, but Operator is built to make dynamic adjustments on the fly. This adaptability is one of the key features that gives it the flexibility to work across industries and handle real-world tasks without constant human intervention.

For example, let's imagine Operator is tasked with booking a flight for a business trip. Initially, the agent might choose a flight based on the user's preferences, such as a specific airline, price range, or travel time. However, if a flight is suddenly canceled due to weather conditions, Operator doesn't simply stop and leave the user in the lurch. Instead, it assesses the situation, looks at alternative options, and presents new flights that match the user's preferences, all while factoring in things like current availability, delays, and potential disruptions. Operator might also consider the user's loyalty to a particular airline or any changes to the user's schedule that might affect their original travel plans. It can even adjust the choice based on the latest data, ensuring that the best possible outcome is achieved without any manual intervention.

Another example of Operator's adaptability can be seen in the world of healthcare. Suppose Operator is managing a medical appointment scheduling system for a hospital. It initially organizes appointments based on available time slots and physician availability. However, if an emergency case arises or a doctor is delayed due to unforeseen circumstances, Operator can quickly adjust the schedule, reassign appointments, and notify patients of changes. The system would automatically prioritize more urgent cases, consider patient preferences, and reschedule the remaining appointments with minimal disruption. If a doctor's schedule changes last minute, Operator can automatically search for the next available qualified specialist and offer patients alternative dates, optimizing the workflow without requiring a human assistant to handle the adjustments manually.

In business operations, where tasks can often become unpredictable, Operator's adaptability shines through when managing project timelines.

Imagine a scenario where a team is working on a large-scale project with tight deadlines. Operator, integrated with the project management software, is responsible for ensuring all tasks are completed on time and within scope. If a task falls behind schedule due to a resource shortage or an unexpected delay, Operator doesn't just flag the delay—it assesses the situation and proposes adjustments. This could involve reallocating resources, shifting priorities, or rescheduling tasks to minimize the impact on the overall timeline. If any further issues arise, like an employee becoming unavailable, Operator can consider alternatives such as outsourcing the task or redistributing workloads among other team members, ensuring the project stays on track.

Operator can also make adjustments when interacting with customers in the service industry. Consider an AI-driven customer service system where a customer is inquiring about a refund or product issue. Operator might initially handle the standard process by requesting order numbers and verifying customer information. However, if the system encounters an issue, such as difficulty verifying the customer's identity due to an input error or a missing detail, Operator doesn't just give up—it adapts to the situation. The agent might ask for additional information, present alternative verification methods, or even direct the customer to a live representative if the issue requires human intervention. In doing so, Operator's flexibility ensures that customer service interactions are smooth, efficient, and resilient, even in the face of unexpected challenges.

In each of these scenarios, the key to Operator's ability to adapt is its reliance on real-time data, probabilistic decision-making, and its ongoing learning process. The system continuously monitors the situation and makes decisions based on the most current information available. Whether it's adjusting for unexpected disruptions or recalculating based on new variables, Operator's adaptability ensures that tasks are completed as efficiently as possible, without manual intervention or excessive back-and-forth. This feature makes it not only a valuable tool in day-to-day operations but also an essential asset in dynamic and fast-paced environments where flexibility is key to success.

As Operator learns from these situations and interacts with users and data, it becomes better at predicting potential issues before they arise. This proactive adaptability gives it a significant edge over traditional AI systems that require constant oversight or manual adjustments. Operator's ability to handle and adjust to unforeseen events with minimal human input demonstrates the true potential of autonomous AI agents in solving real-world problems and optimizing processes across a wide range of industries.

Operator's integration with web browsers marks a major advancement in how AI can streamline and automate tasks directly within the environments where we work and shop. By seamlessly interacting with web pages, Operator removes the need for users to manually navigate between tabs, fill out forms, or even make purchasing decisions. This integration transforms the user experience into a smoother, more efficient process, where the AI is not just assisting, but actively performing tasks that would typically require multiple steps and human effort.

Imagine needing to book a flight. Traditionally, booking a flight involves navigating through several websites, searching for options, comparing prices, selecting dates, inputting personal information, and sometimes even making payments. With Operator, all of this happens within a single web browser window. Operator can open a travel website, scan flight options, filter results based on user preferences (e.g., price range, layovers, preferred airlines), and even make recommendations. Once the user selects a flight, Operator can move between tabs to input the relevant details, such as passenger names, contact information, and payment data. In some cases, the AI might even make the purchase for the user, completing the transaction with the necessary security features in place.

The ability to switch between tabs and perform different tasks simultaneously is crucial to Operator's functionality. For example, after booking a flight, the AI might automatically move to another tab to book a hotel, checking the user's preferences for accommodation type, budget, and location. It can even verify availability and send booking confirmations without any input from the user. If the user has specific requirements—such as needing a pet-friendly hotel or requesting a room with specific amenities—Operator can automatically include these preferences in its search. This seamless, multi-tasking capability extends beyond travel and into various other domains, including shopping, reservations, and workflow management.

Let's say you're shopping online for a new laptop. Operator can analyze the options based on your previous preferences, review ratings, and find the best deals. Once a choice is made, it moves between tabs to complete the purchase, filling in your payment and shipping details, selecting shipping options, and even applying discount codes automatically. It can check out the latest promotional offers or inventory changes and adjust the purchase accordingly, ensuring that you never miss out on a better deal. If you're browsing multiple sites for comparison, Operator can quickly compare prices across vendors and suggest the most cost-effective choice.

This ability to move fluidly between tabs and different websites without constant manual input makes Operator a powerful tool for automating routine tasks. By eliminating the need for a user to actively manage multiple tabs or perform redundant steps, it can save significant amounts of time and effort. Instead of having to log in, check out different options, and manually fill out forms, Operator takes care of it all in the background, functioning like a personal assistant who understands exactly what you need.

What makes this even more impressive is that Operator's adaptability ensures it works with a wide variety of websites, regardless of layout changes or content updates. If a website has a new form layout or a slightly different set of fields, Operator can adjust its approach, recognizing the new structure and responding accordingly. This ability to learn and adapt makes it an ideal solution for tasks that often require a lot of hands-on interaction with websites.

For users, the integration of Operator into web browsers doesn't just simplify tasks—it introduces a new level of convenience and efficiency. It's like having an assistant who is always a step ahead, moving between tabs, completing tasks, and making informed decisions in real-time. Whether it's booking travel arrangements, purchasing items, or handling business workflows, Operator allows users to offload these repetitive tasks to an AI that can execute them with precision, without the need for constant monitoring or intervention.

This deep integration with web browsers also opens up a wide array of possibilities for the future. As AI becomes even more capable of understanding context, preferences, and real-time data, we can imagine scenarios where Operator not only helps complete tasks but also anticipates future needs. If you routinely purchase office supplies, for instance, Operator might automatically reorder items as they run low, adjusting for your current inventory levels. The combination of proactive decision-making and seamless integration with web browsers means that the AI is not just a tool, but an essential, active participant in your daily digital experience.

Chapter 4: Practical Applications of Operator

In the workplace, integrating Operator into daily operations can profoundly change how businesses approach efficiency, productivity, and overall workflow management. Traditionally, employees and managers spend a significant amount of time handling routine tasks such as scheduling meetings, organizing project timelines, managing data, and coordinating across teams. With Operator, many of these time-consuming tasks can be automated, freeing up valuable human resources to focus on more strategic activities that require creative or analytical thinking.

One of the key areas where Operator excels is scheduling. Rather than relying on employees to manually schedule meetings, confirm availability, and resolve scheduling conflicts, Operator can handle all of this autonomously. It can access a company's shared calendar system, understand employees' availability, and arrange meetings based on the most efficient schedules for all parties involved. If conflicts arise, the AI can suggest alternative times, book conference rooms, and even send out meeting invitations automatically, complete with relevant documents or agendas. Operator's ability to automatically sync across multiple calendars ensures that it stays updated on any changes, making scheduling seamless and reducing the risk of double bookings or forgotten appointments.

Operator can also significantly improve data management within an organization. Handling large volumes of data—whether it's customer information, sales reports, or inventory tracking—can be overwhelming. Instead of relying on employees to manually input or update data across various systems, Operator can access the relevant databases and perform updates in real time. For example, if a sales representative submits a report with updated figures, Operator can automatically update the central database, ensure that the report is correctly filed, and send out notifications to relevant stakeholders. This not only speeds up data entry and accuracy but also ensures that everyone in the organization is working with the most current information available.

When it comes to project coordination, Operator can take on the role of a project manager by organizing tasks, assigning responsibilities, and tracking progress. It can monitor project deadlines, identify bottlenecks, and automatically send reminders to team members about upcoming milestones. By analyzing project data and team capacity, Operator can suggest optimal workflows and timelines to help ensure that deadlines are met efficiently. If a task is delayed or requires additional resources, Operator can flag the issue and suggest solutions, such as reassigning tasks or adjusting project priorities.

Operator's adaptability and real-time decision-making capabilities mean that it can handle complex project coordination tasks with ease. For example, if a team encounters an unexpected issue—such as a delay from a vendor or a change in client requirements—Operator can instantly adjust the project's timeline, update all relevant parties, and propose solutions to minimize the impact on the overall project. This kind of agile project management is crucial in today's fast-paced business environment, where quick adjustments and adaptability can make the difference between success and failure.

In addition to these core administrative tasks, Operator can also enhance communication within teams and across departments. For instance, it can monitor project communications, gather key points from email threads or chat discussions, and summarize them for team members. Operator can even suggest or draft responses to common queries, further reducing the time employees spend on repetitive communication tasks. This can be particularly useful in customer support settings, where Operator can autonomously handle routine queries and escalate more complex issues to human agents.

For businesses that require data-driven decision-making, Operator can analyze trends, generate reports, and make data-backed recommendations. By pulling data from multiple sources, it can provide real-time insights into market trends, employee performance, or financial forecasts. This allows business leaders to make informed decisions quickly, without having to sift through piles of data manually.

The integration of Operator into business workflows doesn't just save time; it also reduces the risk of human error. By automating repetitive and detail-oriented tasks, businesses can ensure greater accuracy and consistency across operations. With Operator handling these administrative duties, employees can focus on higher-level tasks that require creativity, critical thinking, and problem-solving.

As businesses continue to embrace digital transformation, integrating AI agents like Operator into the workplace becomes increasingly important. From small startups to large enterprises, every company stands to benefit from the efficiencies that autonomous AI can bring. By adopting systems that can handle scheduling, data management, project coordination, and more, businesses can optimize their workflows, reduce costs, and ultimately boost productivity. Operator isn't just a tool for individual tasks—it's an integral part of an intelligent, connected system that enables businesses to operate more smoothly and effectively.

In everyday life, Operator has the potential to become an indispensable tool for managing the myriad tasks that often overwhelm our personal schedules. From organizing trips to managing emails, and even handling routine chores, Operator's ability to automate and streamline everyday processes can save users significant amounts of time and effort, allowing them to focus on what truly matters.

One of the most practical uses of Operator in personal life is for organizing trips. Planning a vacation or business trip typically involves juggling multiple tasks—booking flights, reserving accommodations, scheduling transport, and finding things to do at the destination. Operator simplifies this process by handling the most time-consuming aspects. It can scan flight options, compare prices, and book the most convenient or cost-effective flights. If you need a hotel, Operator can search through accommodation websites, read reviews, and select a place based on your preferences, availability, and budget. Additionally, Operator can arrange for airport transfers or local transport, ensuring that all logistics are handled seamlessly.

Beyond booking, Operator can manage all the details of a trip. It can create itineraries by finding local attractions, suggesting restaurants, and booking tickets for museums, tours, or events. If your flight is delayed or canceled, Operator can instantly make alternative arrangements, notifying you of updated schedules or suggesting new flight options. By integrating with your calendar and reminder systems, Operator can ensure that you never miss a booking or deadline while on the go.

Operator's adaptability makes it an ideal assistant for managing daily tasks like email organization. With the sheer volume of emails most people receive, it can become overwhelming to keep track of important messages or stay on top of conversations. Operator can scan your inbox, flagging critical emails, sorting them into categories, and even responding to routine queries with pre-programmed replies. If there's an urgent request or a time-sensitive task in an email, Operator can extract the relevant information and create a to-do list or reminder, ensuring nothing slips through the cracks. It can also prioritize messages, helping you stay focused on the most pressing matters first, while delegating less important communications to later in the day.

When it comes to everyday chores, Operator can serve as a personal assistant that takes care of tasks such as managing grocery lists, ordering supplies, or scheduling maintenance appointments. For instance, if you run out of essentials like milk or toilet paper, Operator can automatically add these items to your shopping list or place an order with your preferred online retailer. Similarly, if your home requires repairs or maintenance, Operator can arrange for service appointments, checking availability with trusted local providers, and even confirming service times.

For those who need help staying on top of personal health, Operator can be programmed to track fitness routines, meal plans, or medical appointments. It can remind users to schedule regular check-ups, suggest healthy meal options, or find nearby fitness classes based on personal preferences. By keeping track of your goals,

Operator can offer insights into your progress, helping you stay motivated and organized as you work toward your health objectives.

Another area where Operator excels in everyday life is through task delegation and automation. It can connect to smart home devices to manage household settings, like adjusting the thermostat, controlling lighting, or even managing security systems. If you have a set routine, such as waking up at a specific time or preparing your home for the day, Operator can adjust settings accordingly, creating a smoother, more efficient daily experience.

Operator's ability to integrate across various digital platforms also makes it perfect for organizing and managing finances. It can help with budgeting by analyzing bank transactions, reminding you of upcoming bills, and even suggesting ways to save money based on your spending habits. Additionally, it can help track investments or manage subscriptions, ensuring that all of your financial commitments are up to date.

Perhaps most importantly, Operator's ability to learn and adapt to your specific preferences and needs makes it uniquely suited for personal use. Over time, it can recognize patterns in your behavior, offering smarter, more personalized recommendations. It learns the most efficient ways to handle tasks and can even suggest improvements to your daily routines, optimizing how you spend your time.

As AI continues to evolve, tools like Operator are transforming how we manage our personal lives. What was once a collection of time-consuming tasks can now be handled autonomously by an intelligent agent. From planning a trip to managing your inbox, Operator promises to make life easier, more efficient, and less stressful. It's more than just a virtual assistant—it's an adaptable, proactive companion that helps users reclaim valuable time and stay on top of their busy lives. By automating the mundane and taking care of everyday responsibilities, Operator frees up energy to focus on personal goals, relationships, and the experiences that matter most.

The impact of Operator on various industries could be profound, transforming how businesses operate, interact with customers, and deliver services. By taking on repetitive, time-consuming tasks, Operator frees up human workers to focus on higher-level strategic work, all while improving efficiency and productivity. Here's a closer look at how this powerful AI tool can reshape industries like customer service, healthcare, finance, and software development.

In customer service, Operator has the potential to revolutionize the way companies engage with their customers. Traditionally, customer service representatives handle a wide range of inquiries, from answering product questions to resolving complaints. While chatbots have already begun to assist in this area, Operator takes things to the next level by offering more advanced capabilities. Operator can handle multi-step interactions that go beyond simple queries. For example, if a customer calls in with a problem, Operator can not only understand the issue but also troubleshoot the problem, propose solutions, and even initiate service requests without needing human intervention. It can schedule follow-up calls or emails, track progress, and even send out reminders or updates. Moreover, with its ability to learn and adapt to different customer preferences and scenarios, Operator can offer highly personalized responses, creating a more satisfying customer experience while reducing response times and improving resolution rates.

In the healthcare sector, the potential applications of Operator are numerous. Healthcare professionals often have to manage large amounts of data, from patient histories to treatment plans, medication schedules, and insurance claims. Operator can streamline many of these tasks, enabling more efficient workflows and reducing the risk of human error. For instance, Operator could assist in booking patient appointments, managing patient records, and ensuring follow-up care is scheduled. By automating routine administrative tasks, healthcare providers can focus more on patient care and less on clerical work. Moreover, Operator can help healthcare practitioners make informed decisions by analyzing medical data, identifying trends, and suggesting treatment options based on the latest research. For patients, Operator could act as a personal assistant, tracking medications, setting reminders for doctor's visits, and even suggesting lifestyle changes based on their health data.

The finance industry stands to gain a great deal from AI agents like Operator as well. Operators can manage complex financial tasks such as analyzing market trends, processing transactions, and even providing real-time financial advice. In banking, for instance, Operator could help customers manage their accounts, transfer funds, track expenses, and monitor their credit scores. It could automatically flag irregular transactions and suggest ways to optimize spending or invest more wisely based on financial goals. Investment firms could use Operator to monitor portfolios, assess risk, and provide clients with personalized financial advice, all without the need for constant human oversight. It could even handle administrative tasks such as scheduling meetings, managing client communications, and ensuring compliance with regulatory requirements. With its adaptability, Operator could ensure that financial services are more efficient, accurate, and accessible.

In the realm of software development, Operator offers opportunities to automate many of the repetitive and time-consuming aspects of coding and project management. Software developers often need to manage large codebases, integrate systems, run tests, and deploy updates—all tasks that are ripe for automation. Operator could assist developers by running tests on new code, debugging issues, and even suggesting improvements based on the results. It could automate code reviews, identifying potential flaws or areas for optimization. Additionally, Operator can handle project management tasks, such as scheduling meetings, coordinating with teams, and tracking progress on development cycles. By taking care of the more mundane aspects of software development, Operator allows developers to focus on more creative and high-level aspects of the job, such as designing new features, improving user experiences, and innovating within their field.

The integration of Operator in these industries could lead to significant advancements in productivity, decision-making, and operational efficiency. In customer service, it could reduce wait times and improve satisfaction, while in healthcare, it could enhance patient care and streamline administrative processes. In finance, it could optimize resource management and investment strategies, and in software development, it could lead to faster, more accurate coding and project management. Ultimately, the widespread use of Operator has the potential to reshape the way businesses approach tasks, interact with customers, and deliver services, pushing industries toward a more automated, efficient, and innovative future.

As industries continue to embrace AI agents, Operator stands to be a key player in the transformation of these fields. With its ability to take on complex, multi-step tasks and adapt to real-time data, it offers immense potential to improve operations, reduce costs, and enhance the customer experience. The future of work in these industries may be less about manual tasks and more about collaboration with intelligent, autonomous agents capable of driving innovation and boosting productivity.

Chapter 5: The Future of Work in the Age of AI Agents

The role of AI in automation has long been a topic of debate, particularly when it comes to its potential impact on the workforce. The introduction of autonomous AI agents, like OpenAI's Operator, marks a pivotal shift in this conversation, as these systems are not only capable of assisting in tasks traditionally done by humans but can also replace certain jobs entirely. While automation has been gradually changing industries for years, AI agents like Operator push this trend to a whole new level by handling increasingly complex, multi-step processes that were once thought to require human intervention.

At the core of this change is the fact that AI agents are becoming more autonomous and capable of decision-making, which extends far beyond simple tasks like answering customer service queries or managing schedules. With its ability to manage workflows, make decisions based on real-time data, and even interact with other systems, Operator is capable of performing tasks that would normally require human judgment and expertise. In many cases, this can lead to greater efficiency and productivity, but it also raises questions about the future of work and how automation will affect human workers.

One area where AI agents could make a significant impact is in customer service. While many companies already use chatbots to handle basic inquiries, Operator's ability to manage more complex, multi-step tasks means it could replace human customer service representatives in certain scenarios. For instance, if a customer has an issue that requires troubleshooting, Operator can not only understand the problem but also take the necessary steps to resolve it. It could initiate service requests, schedule follow-up calls, and even send reminders or updates—all without human input. This means fewer customer service representatives would be needed to handle routine inquiries, potentially displacing workers in the process.

In industries like healthcare, where administrative tasks take up a significant portion of professionals' time, AI agents could also replace jobs that are traditionally done by humans. Operator could assist with scheduling, patient record management, and follow-up communications, all of which are typically handled by medical office staff. By taking on these administrative burdens, healthcare workers could focus more on direct patient care, but it could also mean fewer human workers would be needed to support these functions.

In finance, AI agents could automate tasks such as managing accounts, processing transactions, and providing financial advice. For example, Operator could be programmed to monitor market trends, offer investment recommendations, and execute trades—all based on real-time data and algorithms. While financial advisors and analysts might still be needed for more complex tasks, AI agents could replace a large portion of the administrative and data analysis roles that are currently filled by humans. The rise of robo-advisors in the investment world already points to this shift, with AI systems increasingly making investment decisions without human involvement.

Software development, too, stands to be affected by the rise of autonomous AI agents. While human developers will likely remain essential for creative and high-level work, AI agents like Operator could automate many of the routine tasks associated with coding and project management. Tasks such as running tests, debugging code, reviewing documentation, and managing deployment could be handled by AI agents, freeing up developers to focus on more complex and innovative projects. This could lead to increased productivity in software development but also fewer human workers needed to carry out routine tasks.

While there are clear benefits to the automation of these tasks—such as increased efficiency, reduced costs, and the ability to handle more complex problems—the displacement of workers is a real concern. As AI agents take over more responsibilities, many jobs that were once thought to require human intervention could become obsolete. This has sparked concerns about job loss and the broader economic implications of automation. In industries where tasks are repetitive or rule-based, AI agents like Operator may replace a significant portion of the workforce, particularly in customer service, administrative support, and data analysis roles.

However, it is important to recognize that the rise of AI agents also has the potential to create new job opportunities. As businesses adopt AI systems like Operator, there will be an increasing demand for workers who can design, maintain, and manage these AI tools. While some positions may be displaced, new roles in AI development, system management, and oversight will emerge. Workers will need to adapt to the changing landscape by acquiring new skills and knowledge, particularly in fields like machine learning, AI ethics, and automation management.

Moreover, AI's role in automation may not be as binary as it seems. While AI agents will undoubtedly replace certain tasks, they can also serve as valuable tools that augment human workers rather than replace them entirely. In many cases, AI agents like Operator can work alongside humans to improve productivity and decision-making. By handling routine, time-consuming tasks, AI agents allow workers to focus on higher-level activities that require creativity, problem-solving, and emotional intelligence—skills that are more difficult for AI to replicate.

The key to navigating this transition will be ensuring that workers are equipped with the skills needed to thrive in an increasingly automated world. This will require investment in education and training programs that prepare workers for new roles in AI management, data science, and automation oversight. As AI agents like Operator become more integrated into industries, it will be important to create systems that allow humans and AI to work together in a complementary way.

In conclusion, the rise of autonomous AI agents like Operator is a double-edged sword. On one hand, they hold the potential to transform industries, making processes more efficient, reducing costs, and enabling businesses to take on more complex tasks. On the other hand, they could displace workers in roles that have traditionally been filled by humans. While this presents challenges, it also offers opportunities for workers to adapt to new roles and for society to embrace the potential of AI as a tool that enhances human capabilities rather than replacing them entirely. The future of work will likely involve a balance between automation and human expertise, with AI agents acting as partners rather than competitors.

As AI agents like OpenAI's Operator continue to evolve and permeate various industries, they will not only transform existing job roles but also create entirely new career opportunities. The rise of AI brings with it a need for specialized knowledge and skills, leading to the creation of new sectors and positions that did not exist before. While automation may displace some workers, it also has the potential to generate entirely new fields, especially in areas related to AI development, ethical governance, and AI implementation.

One of the most immediate areas of growth will be in AI development itself. As AI agents become more sophisticated and integral to businesses, the demand for professionals skilled in machine learning, natural language processing, and deep learning will soar. These experts will be responsible for developing, training, and improving AI models, ensuring that the systems function correctly and efficiently in real-world applications. Beyond technical roles, the increasing complexity of AI will also create opportunities for specialists in areas like AI system architecture, integration, and optimization, further expanding the pool of career options within the tech industry.

Another key area of opportunity will be in AI ethics and governance. As AI becomes more autonomous, its ability to make decisions that impact individuals and society at large raises critical ethical concerns. For instance, AI systems like Operator will need to make judgments about data privacy, fairness, transparency, and bias. This presents an urgent need for professionals trained in AI ethics to guide the development and implementation of AI technologies. Experts in AI ethics will work with companies, policymakers, and organizations to ensure that AI systems are built and used responsibly, with the highest standards of fairness and accountability.

The governance of AI will also create demand for new roles that bridge the gap between technology and regulation. AI policy experts, legal advisors, and compliance officers will be essential in ensuring that AI systems comply with laws and ethical standards. As governments and international bodies begin to establish regulations for AI, professionals who understand both the technical and legal aspects of AI will be in high demand. These individuals will ensure that AI agents are developed in accordance with best practices and that companies are accountable for their AI-driven decision-making processes.

Additionally, as AI becomes more prevalent in workplaces across all industries, there will be an increasing need for human-centered roles that support the integration of AI into existing systems. AI trainers, system integrators, and process managers will play key roles in helping organizations smoothly transition to AI-driven environments. These professionals will be tasked with implementing AI systems into daily operations, training staff on how to interact with new AI tools, and managing workflows to ensure that AI is used effectively and efficiently.

While AI agents create new job opportunities, it's important to recognize that many workers in industries susceptible to automation may need assistance in transitioning to these emerging roles. As certain tasks become automated, workers in jobs like customer service, administration, data entry, and manual labor may find their roles becoming obsolete or radically changed. This underscores the need for comprehensive worker retraining programs to help employees adapt to the evolving job market.

AI and worker retraining go hand-in-hand in ensuring that individuals who may lose their jobs due to automation have the resources and support to successfully transition into new careers. Retraining programs will be crucial in helping workers learn the skills necessary to thrive in an AI-driven economy. These programs may focus on technical skills like coding, machine learning, and data analysis, but also on softer skills such as critical thinking, creativity, and emotional intelligence—areas where humans continue to excel over machines.

Government and private sector initiatives will be essential in providing funding, resources, and access to these training programs. Many workers, particularly those in low-skill or low-wage jobs, may need financial support or subsidies to afford retraining courses. As industries evolve, it will be important to create pathways for workers to transition into high-demand fields such as healthcare, AI development, cybersecurity, and green energy.

The rise of AI also presents an opportunity to rethink education and workforce development at a more fundamental level. Rather than focusing solely on traditional degree programs, educational systems may need to place greater emphasis on lifelong learning, upskilling, and adaptability. With the rapid pace of technological change, workers must continuously upgrade their skills to stay relevant in the workforce. This will require a shift in how we view career development, with an increasing emphasis on adaptability and continuous learning.

In addition to technical skills, there will also be a demand for professionals who can bridge the gap between humans and machines. As AI systems take over more routine tasks, human workers will increasingly need to focus on higher-level, creative, and strategic work. Roles in management, leadership, and creative fields will still require a human touch, with AI acting as a complementary tool that enhances human decision-making rather than replacing it entirely.

Ultimately, the rise of AI agents like Operator offers a unique opportunity to create a future where technology serves to empower humans, rather than replace them. While automation will undoubtedly change the landscape of work, it also opens the door to new career paths and industries that were once unimaginable. By investing in education, retraining programs, and ethical AI governance, society can help ensure that the workforce is prepared to thrive in an AI-powered world. As we embrace the future of AI, it is crucial that we prioritize human-centric solutions that balance automation with the opportunities for personal growth and career advancement.

Chapter 6: Ethical Considerations of Autonomous AI

As AI systems, particularly autonomous agents like OpenAI's Operator, become more integrated into critical sectors of society, the issue of accountability becomes increasingly complex. These systems are designed to make decisions and take actions without constant human oversight, which introduces new challenges around responsibility when things go wrong. What happens when an AI makes a mistake? Who is to blame if an AI agent operates on faulty or biased data, leading to unintended consequences? These are questions that require careful consideration as AI becomes more autonomous.

AI accountability revolves around the principle that when an AI system causes harm or makes an error, there must be clarity on who is responsible. In the past, accountability was relatively straightforward: if an individual or organization made a mistake, they could be held liable. However, with AI agents, the lines are blurred. When these systems make decisions independently, there are questions about whether the responsibility lies with the AI, the developers who built it, the organizations using it, or even the users interacting with it.

A key issue is that AI systems, especially those based on probabilistic decision-making like Operator, can take actions that are not always predictable or transparent. Unlike traditional software that follows a strict set of rules, AI agents learn from vast amounts of data and make decisions based on probabilities. This makes it difficult to trace the exact cause of an error, especially when the system's actions are based on a combination of multiple data sources and real-time variables. In situations where the AI makes a mistake—such as incorrectly booking a flight or mishandling sensitive data—it may not be immediately obvious where the problem occurred or who is responsible.

One of the core challenges is the issue of data quality. AI agents like Operator rely heavily on the data they are fed, and if that data is inaccurate, incomplete, or biased, the AI's decisions may reflect those flaws. For instance, if an AI system is tasked with analyzing financial data and makes an investment recommendation based on faulty information, the results could be disastrous. The question then becomes: should the blame fall on the AI for acting on bad data, or should the responsibility lie with the developers or data providers who were responsible for ensuring the accuracy of that information?

This dilemma becomes even more pronounced in situations where the AI is acting in a more autonomous, decision-making capacity. If an AI agent handles multiple tasks on behalf of a user—such as scheduling meetings, managing tasks, or making purchases—what happens if it makes a mistake in judgment? Should the user be held accountable, or should the organization that deployed the AI system take responsibility?

The challenge of accountability becomes even more pressing in industries where AI agents are handling critical tasks, such as healthcare or finance. For example, an AI used in a medical setting to assist in diagnosing patients might make a mistake that leads to a missed diagnosis or incorrect treatment plan. If this happens, determining who is responsible is not straightforward. Should the hospital be held liable for deploying the AI? Should the developers of the AI be accountable for its failure to recognize certain medical conditions? Or is the patient responsible for trusting the AI's recommendation?

One potential solution to this issue is transparency. AI systems that operate autonomously need to be transparent about how they make decisions, providing users with insights into the data they are using, the reasoning behind their actions, and the factors influencing their conclusions. This transparency can help users and organizations understand how the AI arrived at its decision, making it easier to trace errors and determine where accountability lies.

To address the issue of AI accountability, some experts believe that there should be a framework for ensuring that AI systems operate within clearly defined ethical and legal boundaries. This could include guidelines for AI developers on how to test, validate, and monitor AI systems to ensure they are functioning as expected. It might also involve creating regulatory bodies that can oversee AI deployment across industries, ensuring that organizations are following best practices for transparency, fairness, and accountability.

In addition to transparency, the use of explainable AI (XAI) is a growing area of focus. XAI refers to AI systems designed to explain their reasoning in ways that humans can understand. This is crucial for building trust in AI and for ensuring that errors can be traced and corrected when they occur. By providing clear explanations of their decision-making processes, AI agents like Operator can help users understand why certain actions were taken, making it easier to hold the system—and those responsible for its deployment—accountable.

AI accountability is also tied to ethical concerns. As AI systems become more autonomous, the potential for them to make biased or harmful decisions grows. For example, if an AI agent is trained on biased data, it may unintentionally perpetuate or exacerbate existing inequalities. This could manifest in a variety of ways: from hiring algorithms that favor one group over another to credit scoring systems that unfairly penalize certain populations. The responsibility for addressing these issues lies not just with the AI developers but with the broader societal structures that govern AI deployment and usage.

As AI continues to evolve and become more integrated into our lives, the need for clear accountability frameworks will only increase. If these systems are to be trusted with significant responsibilities, from healthcare to finance to everyday tasks, we must ensure that there are mechanisms in place to hold AI accountable when it goes wrong. Developing robust frameworks for accountability, improving transparency, and addressing ethical concerns will be crucial in ensuring that AI remains a positive force for innovation and progress, rather than a source of harm and confusion.

As we move towards a future where AI agents like Operator take on increasingly complex and autonomous roles, we will need to develop new standards for AI accountability that align with the capabilities and challenges of these systems. By doing so, we can ensure that AI remains a tool for enhancing human potential, rather than a force that undermines trust or exacerbates harm.

As autonomous AI systems like OpenAI's Operator begin to take on more complex tasks, the handling of sensitive data becomes a significant concern. These AI agents, capable of operating autonomously and making real-time decisions, often need access to vast amounts of personal and private information in order to complete tasks efficiently. Whether it's booking flights, managing emails, or making purchases, AI agents are designed to interact with systems that contain everything from financial data to personal preferences, medical records, and confidential communications. This reliance on sensitive information raises critical questions about privacy and the risks of potential violations.

The central issue surrounding AI and privacy lies in how personal data is accessed, processed, and stored by these systems. Autonomous AI agents typically rely on cloud-based platforms and extensive data sets, meaning the data they interact with could be spread across multiple databases and platforms. This decentralized nature of data handling presents risks related to unauthorized access, misuse, and breaches. In the worst-case scenario, if a vulnerability is exploited, sensitive personal data could be exposed, causing harm to individuals or organizations.

For example, if an AI agent is tasked with managing a user's personal calendar, it may have access to private appointments, sensitive meeting notes, and even health-related data, if the user integrates their calendar with other platforms. If the AI doesn't have strict protocols for data protection, there's the potential for that information to be accessed by unauthorized third parties, either maliciously or accidentally. The risk is even greater if the AI agent interacts with multiple external systems on behalf of the user, as this increases the number of potential touchpoints where sensitive data could be exposed or mishandled.

AI agents like Operator could also inadvertently gather more data than they need to perform a task, leading to situations where private information is collected without explicit consent or understanding. In some cases, users may unknowingly provide more personal data than necessary, which could later be used for purposes beyond their control or approval. As these systems become more autonomous, there's an increasing risk that users might not fully understand the extent of data being collected, or how it's being used, raising concerns about transparency and consent.

This is where privacy protection measures come into play. For AI to be trusted in sensitive applications, strict protocols for data encryption, secure access controls, and transparent data usage policies need to be implemented. Furthermore, these AI systems must be designed to minimize data collection by only requesting or using the information necessary to complete a task. Users should have full control over what data is shared with the AI, as well as the ability to review and delete data if desired. Without these safeguards, there's a risk that the technology could be used in ways that compromise user privacy.

Moreover, as AI agents become more integrated into business operations, the data they handle could have broader implications. For instance, AI in healthcare settings may deal with confidential patient information, while in finance, it could interact with financial records and transaction data. In these contexts, a breach of privacy could have serious consequences, not just for the individual user, but for entire organizations and industries. AI systems must therefore adhere to stringent privacy standards, especially in sectors that handle particularly sensitive data, like healthcare, finance, and law.

This brings us to the larger issue of transparency in AI systems. As AI becomes more capable, it's essential that these systems operate transparently, offering clear visibility into how data is being used, processed, and stored. Users should have a comprehensive understanding of the types of data the AI interacts with, and what it does with that information once the task is completed. Transparency can help mitigate concerns about privacy violations by enabling users to see exactly how their data is being handled at every stage.

Transparency is also critical in the development and deployment of AI systems. Developers and organizations using AI agents need to provide clear explanations of the decision-making processes behind these systems, including how and why they access certain data, and how that data is being protected. This openness helps build trust with users and ensures that AI systems operate within agreed-upon ethical boundaries. Transparency also makes it easier to detect and correct issues when they arise, particularly in cases where privacy concerns are implicated.

However, transparency alone is not enough. Regulation is needed to ensure that AI systems operate responsibly and ethically. Governments and regulatory bodies around the world are already beginning to examine how AI should be governed, with some countries enacting laws and regulations to ensure that AI systems protect user privacy and data security. In the European Union, for example, the General Data Protection Regulation (GDPR) sets strict standards for how personal data can be collected and used, including rules for AI systems that handle sensitive information. Such regulations are a step in the right direction, but more work needs to be done to address the unique challenges posed by autonomous AI systems.

The challenge is that AI is evolving so rapidly that existing privacy laws and frameworks may not always be sufficient to address emerging concerns. As AI continues to integrate into more aspects of daily life, it will be crucial to develop new guidelines that specifically address the risks and challenges posed by autonomous agents. These guidelines should focus on ensuring that AI systems are designed to prioritize user privacy and security, while also providing mechanisms for accountability in the event of data breaches or misuse.

As AI technology continues to advance, the responsibility for safeguarding privacy will rest not only on the developers of AI systems but also on the companies and industries that deploy them. It will be important for all stakeholders to work together to create a comprehensive framework for ensuring that AI operates in a way that is not only effective and efficient but also ethical and respectful of user privacy.

In conclusion, privacy concerns are an integral part of the conversation surrounding autonomous AI agents. As AI systems like Operator become more capable of handling sensitive data and performing complex tasks, ensuring that users' privacy is protected will be a critical challenge. Transparency and regulation are key to mitigating the risks associated with AI's use of personal information, and it will be up to developers, organizations, and regulators to create clear guidelines that ensure AI systems operate responsibly and ethically. With the right safeguards in place, AI can be a powerful tool for enhancing productivity and improving lives, without compromising user privacy.

Chapter 7: The Business Implications of Operator

Businesses today face the challenge of balancing productivity with cost-efficiency. In an increasingly competitive market, finding ways to reduce manual work, minimize errors, and streamline operations has become a priority. OpenAI's Operator, with its advanced capabilities as an autonomous AI agent, offers a transformative solution for organizations looking to optimize their workflows. By integrating Operator into their systems, businesses can automate routine tasks, reduce the need for human intervention, and improve overall efficiency in ways that were previously impossible.

One of the key advantages of using Operator is its ability to handle repetitive, time-consuming tasks with high accuracy. Tasks such as data entry, scheduling, managing emails, and customer service inquiries often require significant manual effort and can be prone to human error. For instance, an employee tasked with managing customer service tickets might struggle with prioritizing requests, leading to delays or overlooked issues. By automating this process, Operator can quickly sort, categorize, and respond to inquiries, ensuring that no task is missed, and reducing the chances of costly mistakes.

In the case of data management, many businesses struggle with keeping records up to date, entering data accurately, and analyzing large sets of information. Manual data entry not only consumes valuable time but is also prone to human errors, which can lead to inconsistencies and mistakes that impact decision-making. Operator's ability to autonomously interact with databases, update records, and process information without direct human input can greatly reduce the margin for error. This results in more reliable data and frees up employees to focus on more strategic, high-value tasks that require human insight and creativity.

Furthermore, Operator's efficiency can drastically cut down on operational costs. By automating workflows, businesses can eliminate the need for extensive manual labor in administrative roles, reducing overhead costs associated with hiring and training additional staff. This also leads to a more agile business model, where operations can scale without a proportional increase in workforce size. With less reliance on manual processes, businesses can also reduce the risk of delays and disruptions, improving overall operational agility.

Another area where Operator can provide significant value is in reducing human error. While humans are highly capable, the pressure of juggling multiple tasks, tight deadlines, and distractions can lead to mistakes. These errors, no matter how small, can accumulate over time and have a significant impact on business operations. Operator's ability to consistently perform tasks with high accuracy and reliability means that businesses can reduce the likelihood of errors that could result in financial losses, customer dissatisfaction, or reputational damage.

For instance, in industries like finance, where precision is crucial, even a small mistake in data entry can lead to major consequences. Operator can assist in processing financial transactions, updating client records, and generating reports with minimal risk of human oversight, ensuring that all information is accurate and up-to-date. This reduction in errors, coupled with the speed at which Operator can complete tasks, enhances overall productivity and ensures that business operations run smoothly.

Moreover, the integration of Operator into business operations can also help streamline communication and collaboration. With the ability to manage emails, coordinate meeting schedules, and track project deadlines, businesses can improve internal coordination and reduce the chances of missed communications or scheduling conflicts. For teams working on complex projects with multiple stakeholders, Operator can automate reminders, send updates, and track progress, ensuring that everyone is aligned and on schedule.

Ultimately, Operator allows businesses to operate more efficiently by reducing the time spent on manual, repetitive tasks and reallocating resources to more impactful areas. This efficiency gain is particularly valuable for small businesses or startups that may not have the budget for large teams. By leveraging Operator's capabilities, these organizations can level the playing field, automating processes that would otherwise require significant human resources.

Beyond efficiency and cost savings, the data-driven insights provided by Operator can also help businesses optimize their operations further. By analyzing patterns and trends in the tasks it handles, Operator can identify bottlenecks, areas of inefficiency, or opportunities for improvement. For example, it might flag tasks that consistently take longer than expected, suggest alternative workflows, or highlight areas where additional automation could provide even greater benefits. This kind of insight is invaluable for businesses seeking continuous improvement in their operations.

Moreover, with the ability to scale operations without additional manual labor, businesses can expand more easily, handling larger volumes of work without the need to hire more staff or invest in costly infrastructure. Whether it's processing more customer service tickets, managing larger project portfolios, or handling more complex data analysis tasks, Operator's scalability ensures that businesses can keep pace with growing demands without compromising quality or efficiency.

In summary, the integration of OpenAI's Operator can help businesses reduce manual work, minimize human error, and significantly improve operational efficiency. By automating repetitive tasks, increasing accuracy, and streamlining workflows, businesses can save time and money while increasing productivity. Operator's ability to adapt to real-time situations and handle complex tasks with minimal human intervention makes it a powerful tool for organizations looking to optimize their operations and stay competitive in an increasingly automated world.

In the ever-evolving world of customer service, businesses are increasingly turning to AI to meet the growing demands for efficiency, speed, and personalization. One of the most promising advancements in this space is the use of autonomous AI agents like OpenAI's Operator, which can revolutionize how companies handle customer queries, manage service tickets, and enhance overall client experiences. By seamlessly integrating AI into customer service operations, businesses can offer faster response times, reduce costs, and improve satisfaction, all while maintaining a high level of accuracy and consistency.

Operator's ability to manage customer service tickets is a key aspect of its potential impact.

Traditionally, service teams must sift through large volumes of incoming requests, prioritize them based on urgency, and respond individually to each one. This process is not only time-consuming but also leaves room for human error, leading to miscommunications, delays, or overlooked inquiries. Operator, however, can autonomously sort and prioritize tickets based on pre-set criteria or customer urgency, ensuring that the most critical issues are addressed first. By automating this process, businesses can ensure faster resolution times and reduce the burden on human service representatives, allowing them to focus on more complex issues that require human empathy and problem-solving.

Furthermore, Operator's ability to handle routine customer queries is another way it can streamline customer service operations. For common questions such as product inquiries, return policies, or order status, Operator can provide immediate responses, offering customers the information they need without having to wait for a human representative. This not only enhances the customer experience by offering instant support but also frees up human agents to address more complex or nuanced concerns. Whether it's answering frequently asked questions or providing troubleshooting advice, Operator's conversational AI capabilities ensure that customers receive prompt and accurate responses, no matter the time of day.

But what truly sets Operator apart is its ability to engage in more dynamic and context-aware conversations. Unlike static chatbots that follow rigid scripts, Operator's ability to adapt and make decisions based on real-time data allows it to engage in more fluid, natural exchanges with customers. If a customer presents a unique or complex issue, Operator can seamlessly pivot the conversation, gather additional details, and escalate the matter to a human agent when needed. This flexibility ensures that customer interactions feel personalized and responsive, reducing frustration and building trust between the business and its clientele.

Moreover, the potential for AI agents like Operator to provide personalized customer experiences is immense. By integrating with customer relationship management (CRM) systems, Operator can access detailed customer histories, preferences, and previous interactions. This allows it to tailor responses and recommendations to individual needs, providing a level of personalization that is often difficult to achieve with human agents alone. For example, if a customer asks about a product they've previously purchased, Operator can offer tailored suggestions based on that purchase history or alert the customer about related products or updates. This personalized approach not only improves the customer experience but also opens up opportunities for cross-selling and upselling, boosting sales for the business.

Operator's adaptability also extends to handling various communication channels. Whether it's email, live chat, social media, or even phone calls, Operator can seamlessly transition between different platforms, providing consistent service across all touchpoints. This ensures that customers have a unified experience regardless of how they choose to interact with the business. It also enables businesses to maintain a presence across multiple channels without the need for a large, dedicated team to monitor and respond to each one individually. This level of automation allows businesses to stay engaged with customers 24/7, meeting the growing demand for around-the-clock service and support.

For businesses in highly competitive industries, the ability to offer quick and efficient customer service can be a game-changer. In the past, long wait times or inconsistent service could drive customers to competitors. With Operator, businesses can drastically reduce response times and ensure that customers are consistently satisfied with the level of support they receive. The AI agent's ability to handle multiple requests simultaneously means that no customer will be left waiting for long periods, even during peak times. This helps maintain customer loyalty, improves retention rates, and contributes to overall brand reputation.

Beyond improving efficiency and response times, AI agents like Operator can also be invaluable in gathering insights about customer behavior and preferences. Every interaction with a customer provides valuable data that can be analyzed to uncover trends, pain points, and areas for improvement. By leveraging this data, businesses can optimize their customer service processes, fine-tune their product offerings, and identify emerging issues before they become widespread problems. Additionally, by tracking and analyzing customer sentiment through natural language processing (NLP), Operator can help businesses gauge overall customer satisfaction and adjust their strategies accordingly.

Operator's role in improving customer service is not just about reducing costs and increasing speed; it's about creating a more engaging and dynamic experience for customers. By handling repetitive tasks, offering personalized recommendations, and providing timely support, AI agents like Operator allow businesses to focus on building stronger relationships with their clients. Whether it's resolving issues, providing information, or engaging in meaningful conversations, AI has the potential to redefine how companies interact with their customers, ultimately leading to more satisfied and loyal clients.

In summary, AI agents like OpenAI's Operator have the potential to revolutionize customer service by automating routine tasks, managing service tickets, offering personalized interactions, and improving operational efficiency. As businesses adopt these technologies, they will not only reduce costs and enhance productivity but also create a more positive and responsive customer experience. The future of customer service is moving toward a more AI-driven model, where businesses can provide fast, accurate, and personalized support to their clients with minimal human intervention. With Operator, that future is already becoming a reality.

Integrating AI agents like OpenAI's Operator into a company's existing tech stack is one of the key challenges and opportunities in adopting this advanced technology. However, the beauty of Operator lies in its ability to integrate seamlessly with a variety of existing tools and platforms, enabling businesses to leverage their current infrastructure while enhancing it with powerful AI capabilities. Whether it's through customer relationship management (CRM) systems, project management platforms, email clients, or communication tools, Operator is designed to fit into the daily workflows that companies already rely on.

One of the core strengths of Operator is its versatility in working with both cloud-based and on-premise software solutions. It can integrate with popular CRM systems like Salesforce or HubSpot, allowing businesses to streamline customer service interactions, manage leads, and track customer histories without requiring a major overhaul of their existing setup. For instance, Operator can pull customer data directly from a CRM system to provide personalized responses to inquiries, offer product recommendations based on past purchases, or even schedule follow-up tasks for sales teams. This integration ensures that the AI agent adds value without disrupting the company's established processes, making it easier to adopt and scale.

Moreover, Operator is capable of integrating with project management and productivity platforms like Trello, Asana, or Jira, enabling teams to automate task creation, track project progress, and facilitate collaboration. For example, when a new task is assigned, Operator can automatically send reminders, update project statuses, or even assign tasks to the appropriate team members based on predefined rules. This removes the need for manual task management, reducing administrative overhead and improving team efficiency. With the ability to pull data from these platforms in real-time, Operator ensures that teams are always aligned and up to date, making collaboration smoother and faster.

In the world of communication, Operator can be integrated into platforms like Slack, Microsoft Teams, and Zoom, enabling companies to automate messages, respond to inquiries, and even schedule meetings. Instead of relying on human agents to manage these communications, Operator can handle routine messages, respond to frequently asked questions, and even engage in dynamic conversations with employees or customers. This integration with communication platforms enhances internal workflows and ensures that important messages are never missed, whether in the form of chat notifications, reminders, or task updates.

Another significant advantage of Operator is its ability to interface with e-commerce platforms such as Shopify, Magento, and WooCommerce. This allows businesses to automate key aspects of the customer experience, such as order processing, inventory management, and product recommendations. For example, if a customer inquires about the availability of a particular product, Operator can check inventory levels, process the order, and even suggest related items based on customer preferences. By automating these routine processes, businesses can increase operational efficiency and reduce the likelihood of human error, all while improving the customer experience with faster responses and better service.

Operator's integration capabilities extend beyond just customer-facing platforms. It can work with back-end systems such as accounting software, enterprise resource planning (ERP) systems, and data management tools. For example, when a financial report is due, Operator can automatically gather data from accounting software, process the necessary information, and generate the report with minimal human input. It can also interact with ERP systems to ensure that supply chain management, inventory control, and order fulfillment are running smoothly. This integration helps businesses streamline their back-end operations, reduce bottlenecks, and ensure that critical data is always up to date and accessible.

In addition to these pre-existing integrations, Operator can be customized to work with other niche tools or proprietary systems that a company might use. Its modular design and API (Application Programming Interface) capabilities allow businesses to tailor the AI agent to their specific needs, integrating it with in-house applications or third-party services that are essential to their operations. This flexibility makes Operator a highly adaptable solution for businesses in various industries, from retail and finance to healthcare and education.

The process of integrating Operator into a company's existing tech stack typically involves several steps. First, businesses need to evaluate their current software ecosystem to identify the tools and platforms that would benefit most from automation and AI-driven enhancements. Once the integrations are determined, a technical team can configure Operator to work with those systems, often leveraging APIs or pre-built connectors to ensure smooth communication between the platforms. Training the AI model to understand company-specific workflows and data is another crucial step in ensuring that Operator functions as intended.

Once integrated, the impact of Operator on the tech stack is immediate and significant. By automating routine tasks, reducing manual effort, and enhancing decision-making capabilities, businesses can achieve higher levels of productivity and operational efficiency. Furthermore, by streamlining processes across different departments—whether it's sales, marketing, customer service, or finance—Operator ensures that all teams are working with the same accurate and up-to-date information, promoting better coordination and collaboration.

A key benefit of integrating Operator with existing platforms is that it doesn't require businesses to abandon their current tools or processes. Instead, it enhances and automates them, allowing companies to maintain their operational continuity while benefiting from the advanced capabilities of AI. This approach reduces the friction typically associated with adopting new technologies and ensures a smoother transition to more automated, AI-powered workflows.

Furthermore, as companies continue to expand their use of AI, they can scale Operator's capabilities to accommodate more complex tasks and larger volumes of data. With the ability to process and analyze vast amounts of information in real-time, Operator can evolve with the business, taking on more responsibilities as the company grows. Whether it's automating customer support, managing internal operations, or driving strategic decision-making, Operator's adaptability ensures that businesses can rely on it for a wide range of tasks.

In summary, integrating Operator into a company's existing tech stack is a seamless process that leverages the power of AI to enhance existing systems. By connecting with popular platforms and tools across various departments—such as CRM, project management, communication, e-commerce, and back-end systems—Operator can streamline workflows, improve productivity, and reduce manual effort. This integration not only enhances business operations but also allows companies to adopt AI technology without disrupting their established processes. Operator's versatility and adaptability make it a powerful tool for businesses looking to unlock the potential of AI in their daily operations, now and in the future.

Chapter 8: The Environmental Impact of AI

The energy consumption of AI systems has become an increasingly significant concern as AI technology continues to advance and models grow larger and more complex. While the potential for AI to revolutionize industries and improve efficiencies is undeniable, the environmental impact of running these systems cannot be overlooked. The computational power required to train and deploy large-scale AI models, such as OpenAI's Operator, demands significant amounts of energy. This energy usage comes from the powerful servers and data centers that host these models, which require extensive cooling, storage, and processing capabilities to handle the vast amounts of data involved.

Training a single large AI model can consume as much energy as several hundred homes would use in a year, and running these models in real-time to serve billions of queries and process data can generate a continuous demand for energy. The need for highly sophisticated hardware and vast computing power makes the energy footprint of AI a critical issue for both developers and businesses looking to scale AI applications. As AI becomes more embedded into everyday business operations, from automating workflows to providing customer support, the demand for power to run these systems will only increase.

The growing energy needs of AI systems are leading to greater scrutiny of the sources of energy used to power these massive computing resources. Traditionally, data centers have relied heavily on fossil fuels for their electricity needs, contributing to carbon emissions and environmental degradation. However, as awareness of the environmental impact of AI grows, there is increasing pressure on companies, tech giants, and AI developers to find more sustainable solutions. To address this issue, there is a growing movement within the tech industry to prioritize renewable energy sources, such as wind, solar, and hydropower, to reduce the carbon footprint associated with AI.

Several leading tech companies, including Google, Microsoft, and Amazon, have committed to transitioning their data centers to 100% renewable energy. Google, for instance, has made significant strides in using renewable energy for its data centers, and Microsoft has announced plans to become carbon-negative by 2030. These companies are leading the way in showing that it is possible to power AI models and data centers using cleaner energy, which is crucial for mitigating the environmental impact of AI technologies.

For AI developers and businesses incorporating AI systems like Operator into their operations, it is important to consider the environmental impact and seek ways to reduce energy consumption. One approach is to optimize AI models to be more energy-efficient, ensuring that they require less computational power to perform tasks. Techniques like model pruning, quantization, and knowledge distillation can help reduce the size and complexity of AI models, making them less resource-intensive while maintaining performance.

Additionally, businesses can explore the possibility of running AI models in hybrid environments that combine on-premise infrastructure with cloud-based solutions. By distributing computational tasks across multiple sources, including renewable-powered cloud data centers, businesses can strike a balance between performance and sustainability. Using edge computing, where data is processed closer to the source rather than being transmitted to distant servers, is another potential strategy for reducing energy consumption. Edge computing can help minimize the need for long-distance data transmission, thus lowering the energy costs associated with running AI systems.

As the demand for AI continues to grow, the need for sustainable energy practices will only intensify.

AI developers and businesses must recognize the importance of balancing innovation with environmental responsibility. By prioritizing the use of renewable energy, optimizing AI systems for energy efficiency, and adopting sustainable practices, the AI industry can continue to advance without compromising the planet's well-being. The future of AI should not only focus on making these systems smarter but also on making them more sustainable, ensuring that their benefits extend to both businesses and the environment.

In the long term, the integration of renewable energy and the continued optimization of AI models for efficiency will be key to ensuring that AI technologies like Operator can thrive while minimizing their environmental impact. As the industry moves forward, creating AI that is both intelligent and energy-conscious will be essential for its continued growth and widespread adoption.

As the AI industry continues to grow, sustainability has become an increasingly important issue. The environmental footprint of AI, particularly in terms of energy consumption and carbon emissions, is drawing heightened attention. While AI models like OpenAI's Operator are pushing the boundaries of what is possible in technology, they also come with significant environmental costs due to the computational power required to train and operate them. This has led to a growing demand within the industry to address these concerns and find ways to make AI more sustainable.

One of the key ways the AI industry is working toward sustainability is by transitioning to renewable energy sources to power AI models and data centers. OpenAI, like many other leading tech companies, recognizes the need for a more sustainable approach and has made strides in adopting green energy practices. While specific details about OpenAI's energy use are not always publicly available, the company has expressed its commitment to reducing its environmental impact and supports the broader movement within the tech industry toward carbon-neutral operations.

The use of renewable energy to power AI infrastructure is crucial for minimizing the environmental costs associated with these powerful technologies. By relying on wind, solar, and other renewable energy sources, AI companies can significantly reduce the carbon emissions generated by their data centers. This shift towards sustainable energy not only helps combat climate change but also sets a standard for the entire AI and tech industries to follow.

Leading tech giants like Google and Microsoft are setting an example by achieving ambitious renewable energy goals. Google, for instance, has been operating on 100% renewable energy since 2017 and continues to push the envelope on sustainability. Microsoft has pledged to become carbon negative by 2030, meaning it plans to remove more carbon from the atmosphere than it emits. These companies' efforts to run data centers on renewable energy and invest in energy-efficient technologies are setting the stage for a more sustainable AI industry.

In addition to adopting renewable energy, AI companies are also exploring ways to make their models more efficient, thus reducing the overall energy consumption required for training and deployment. One approach is through the use of more energy-efficient hardware, such as custom-designed chips optimized for AI processing. These chips can perform complex AI tasks while consuming less power compared to traditional processors. AI developers are also focusing on algorithmic optimizations that allow models to perform at a high level with fewer resources. Techniques like model pruning, where unnecessary parameters are removed from a model, and knowledge distillation, where large models are compressed into smaller, more efficient versions, help reduce energy consumption.

Looking to the future, the development of AI systems that are both powerful and energy-efficient is becoming a central focus of the industry. One promising approach is the integration of AI with edge computing, where data is processed closer to where it is generated rather than being sent to distant data centers for processing. This reduces the need for long-distance data transmission, which can be energy-intensive, and lowers the overall energy cost of running AI systems. By processing data locally on devices like smartphones, smart home devices, and even autonomous vehicles, edge computing could help reduce the energy burden on central data centers.

The future of sustainable AI also includes innovations in AI model design and the development of more efficient algorithms. Researchers are working on creating AI models that require fewer training steps and can learn more efficiently from smaller datasets. This could drastically reduce the computational resources required for training large-scale models and minimize the environmental impact.

Furthermore, the rise of "green AI" initiatives, where researchers and developers prioritize sustainability as a core aspect of their AI work, will help accelerate the shift toward more environmentally conscious AI practices. By developing AI models that are not only effective but also energy-efficient, the industry can ensure that AI continues to grow while minimizing its impact on the planet.

In addition to these technical advances, the AI industry must continue to collaborate with policymakers and environmental organizations to establish regulations and guidelines that promote sustainability. Creating industry-wide standards for carbon emissions, energy efficiency, and the use of renewable energy in AI operations will be essential for scaling AI technology without compromising the environment.

The future of AI is not just about making smarter, more capable systems; it's about creating AI that can operate sustainably and with minimal impact on the planet. As the AI industry moves forward, it must balance innovation with responsibility, ensuring that the benefits of artificial intelligence can be enjoyed without contributing to environmental degradation. By embracing renewable energy, optimizing models for efficiency, and investing in sustainable practices, the AI industry can help build a future where technology and the environment coexist harmoniously, allowing AI to thrive in a way that benefits both businesses and the planet.

Chapter 9: Accessibility and the Democratization of AI

As artificial intelligence continues to evolve and become a powerful tool across industries, there is growing concern about the exclusivity of these technologies. AI, particularly advanced systems like OpenAI's Operator, requires significant computational resources and infrastructure to develop and operate. As a result, there is a real risk that these powerful AI tools could be concentrated in the hands of large corporations with the financial means to afford and leverage them, while small businesses and individual users may be left behind.

The accessibility gap between large corporations and smaller entities is not new, but AI has the potential to exacerbate this divide. While large companies have the resources to develop, deploy, and scale AI solutions that can automate processes, improve efficiencies, and innovate products, small businesses and individuals may struggle to keep up. The costs associated with acquiring, implementing, and maintaining AI systems can be prohibitive, especially for startups or small companies with limited budgets.

This disparity in access to AI technologies could have significant implications for competition and innovation. Large corporations with access to sophisticated AI tools may be able to streamline their operations, reduce costs, and offer improved products and services at a scale that smaller competitors cannot match. This could lead to a concentration of power and influence within a few key players in the industry, stifling competition and innovation in the long term.

Moreover, AI tools that are primarily developed for the needs of large enterprises may not be suitable or scalable for smaller businesses, which often require more specialized or customizable solutions. For example, while AI-driven customer service systems might work well for a multinational corporation handling millions of customers, a small local business may not need the same level of automation or complexity. This mismatch in scale and functionality could prevent smaller companies from realizing the full benefits of AI.

In addition to businesses, there is also concern about the accessibility of AI for individual users. As AI systems like Operator evolve, they become increasingly capable of handling complex tasks and making decisions autonomously. However, these systems are often hosted on cloud platforms and require specialized knowledge to use effectively. Individuals without the technical skills or resources to integrate AI into their personal or professional lives may find themselves at a disadvantage. This exclusion could deepen the digital divide, with those who can afford AI tools reaping the benefits, while those who cannot are left behind.

There is also the ethical question of whether AI, as it becomes more powerful and pervasive, should be controlled and regulated in such a way that ensures equal access for everyone, regardless of their size or resources. The growing reliance on AI in industries like healthcare, finance, and education makes it essential that these tools are not monopolized by a few large players, but are accessible to a broader range of businesses and individuals. Without proper oversight, there is a risk that AI will only serve to widen the gap between the haves and have-nots.

The potential for AI exclusivity has prompted calls for greater regulation and advocacy for equal access to AI technologies. Some experts argue that governments and international bodies should intervene to ensure that AI remains a tool for progress and innovation that benefits society as a whole, rather than just a select few. This could include policies that promote open-source AI initiatives, subsidies or grants for small businesses to adopt AI technologies, and support for educational programs that help individuals gain the necessary skills to work with AI.

In the future, the development of AI tools that are specifically designed to be accessible, scalable, and cost-effective for smaller businesses and individuals will be crucial for ensuring that the benefits of AI are shared more widely. OpenAI's approach to offering API access to models like GPT-3 and Operator, which allow businesses of all sizes to integrate AI into their operations, is a step in the right direction. By making these powerful tools available to a broader audience, OpenAI is helping to level the playing field and democratize access to AI.

Ultimately, the challenge will be to create an AI ecosystem that encourages innovation and competition without leaving certain groups behind. This will require collaboration between businesses, governments, and regulators to ensure that the development of AI technologies is guided by principles of fairness, transparency, and inclusivity. By addressing the risk of AI exclusivity head-on, we can build an AI-powered future that benefits everyone, not just the largest corporations.

As artificial intelligence continues to advance, there is an increasing push to make these transformative technologies more accessible to everyone. The growing concern over AI exclusivity has prompted both private companies and governments to explore ways to democratize AI and ensure that it benefits a broader range of users, from large corporations to small businesses and individual users.

One of the most significant efforts to make AI more accessible comes from open-source projects. These initiatives allow developers and businesses of all sizes to access and contribute to AI technologies without the barriers of high licensing fees or proprietary restrictions. By providing the source code for free or at a low cost, open-source projects enable anyone with the right skills to customize, implement, and scale AI solutions to suit their specific needs.

Microsoft's **Magentic 1** project is an excellent example of this shift. Magentic 1 is designed to provide smaller businesses with a lightweight, accessible AI agent that can handle a variety of tasks, from data analysis to workflow automation. Unlike traditional enterprise-level AI solutions, which are often expensive and require substantial infrastructure, Magentic 1 is designed to be used by businesses of all sizes, including startups and small enterprises. Its open-source nature means that developers can modify the code to suit their specific needs, allowing for greater flexibility and customization.

Similarly, **Google** is working on its own AI agents that aim to serve as accessible, scalable solutions for a wider range of users. The upcoming Google AI agents will be integrated into various Google platforms, offering users the ability to leverage powerful AI tools within existing applications. These agents are being designed with the goal of reducing the technical barriers to AI adoption, allowing small businesses and individuals to harness AI's potential without needing specialized knowledge or resources.

These open-source projects and initiatives are part of a broader movement within the tech industry to make AI more inclusive. By lowering the cost of entry and making the underlying technologies more transparent, companies like Microsoft and Google are helping to level the playing field. Smaller businesses can now adopt AI tools without having to invest heavily in research and development or infrastructure. This has the potential to spark innovation, as companies with limited resources can still leverage AI to improve their products, services, and workflows.

However, open-source projects alone may not be enough to ensure that AI technologies are accessible to everyone. Government initiatives and policies will play a crucial role in promoting equitable access to advanced AI tools. Many governments around the world are starting to recognize the importance of AI and its potential to transform industries, and are taking steps to ensure that the benefits of AI are distributed fairly.

One example of such a policy initiative is the European Union's **AI Act**, which aims to establish clear regulations for the development and use of AI technologies. The AI Act focuses on promoting transparency, accountability, and fairness in AI systems, while also ensuring that AI remains accessible to businesses of all sizes. By regulating the use of AI and setting standards for safety, ethics, and transparency, the EU hopes to create an environment where AI technologies are not only safe and effective but also available to a wide range of users.

In the United States, the **National AI Initiative Act** was signed into law to promote AI research and development, with a focus on making AI accessible to various sectors, including healthcare, education, and manufacturing. This initiative includes funding for AI research, as well as programs aimed at training the workforce to meet the growing demand for AI-related jobs. It also emphasizes the need for ethical guidelines and regulations to ensure that AI technologies are developed in a way that benefits society as a whole.

Beyond specific pieces of legislation, there is also growing recognition of the importance of **AI literacy** and workforce development. Governments are increasingly focused on programs that help individuals acquire the skills needed to work with AI technologies. Whether through public education systems, vocational training, or partnerships with tech companies, these initiatives aim to ensure that workers are equipped with the skills necessary to navigate the AI-driven economy. This will be essential for ensuring that workers are not left behind as AI becomes more integrated into every aspect of society.

Moreover, international collaboration is essential for ensuring that AI remains accessible globally, particularly in developing countries. Many countries lack the resources to develop their own AI solutions, and without access to advanced AI tools, they risk falling behind economically. Global initiatives, such as those led by the **United Nations** and other international organizations, aim to promote collaboration and knowledge-sharing in AI development, ensuring that emerging economies have access to the same technologies as wealthier nations.

Ultimately, the goal is to create a world where AI is not just a tool for the wealthy and powerful, but a resource that everyone can access and use to improve their lives. The efforts of companies like Microsoft, Google, and others, combined with government policies that promote equity and inclusivity, are paving the way for a future where AI is widely accessible, transparent, and used responsibly.

By fostering collaboration between the public and private sectors, encouraging open-source development, and creating policies that ensure fairness, we can build a more inclusive AI ecosystem. In doing so, we can ensure that AI benefits everyone, regardless of their resources or background, and contributes to the creation of a more equitable and prosperous society.

Chapter 10: What's Next for AI Agents?

As the development of autonomous AI agents progresses, the future promises even more sophisticated systems capable of transforming industries and personal experiences in ways we've only begun to imagine. OpenAI's **Operator** represents just the first step in a larger evolution of AI technology, and the question on everyone's mind is: What comes next?

In the coming years, we can expect AI agents to grow exponentially in their abilities and applications, becoming more integrated into our daily lives and workplaces. The next generation of AI agents will not only be able to handle more complex tasks but also function with greater autonomy, adaptability, and intelligence, transforming them into more intuitive, proactive assistants.

One key area where we will see advancement is in the **integration of multimodal capabilities**.

While current AI agents like Operator can handle specific tasks such as booking flights or managing workflows, future AI agents will likely be able to process and synthesize information across multiple forms of data—such as images, video, audio, and text—allowing them to perform tasks that require a broader understanding of the world around them. These agents will not just respond to text-based inputs; they will have the capability to analyze and interpret visual content, make sense of voice interactions, and understand complex, context-sensitive cues. This would allow users to interact with their AI agents in more natural and dynamic ways, making them far more versatile and adaptable to the complexity of real-world scenarios.

Along with increased multimodal capabilities, we can expect **AI agents to become more deeply embedded into our digital and physical environments**. As AI systems advance, they will interact more seamlessly with the world around them. From smart homes to augmented reality environments, the AI of the future will likely be embedded in our physical spaces, managing everything from climate control to security and even assisting with home-based tasks. These AI agents will work across connected devices, interacting with everything from household appliances to personal gadgets, creating a more automated and efficient lifestyle.

Another significant development will be the **improved use of natural language processing (NLP) and contextual understanding**. Current AI agents are fairly good at responding to queries and executing commands, but they are still limited in their ability to understand context on a deeper level. Future agents will be able to hold more fluid, continuous conversations with users, understanding context, emotional tone, and intent more accurately. This will allow AI agents to take on more nuanced roles, whether it's in customer service, healthcare, education, or personal assistance, where the human touch and emotional intelligence are just as important as functionality.

Ethical and responsible AI will also be a central focus in the development of future agents. As AI systems become more powerful and autonomous, ensuring that they operate within ethical boundaries and align with human values will be critical. The future of AI will likely involve ongoing research into creating systems that can reason and make decisions in ways that reflect not just logical outcomes but also fairness, inclusivity, and social good. We can expect AI developers to place a greater emphasis on transparency, accountability, and bias mitigation in the design of future AI agents.

Furthermore, **AI's ability to collaborate with humans** will evolve from being purely task-based into more collaborative partnerships. Instead of simply following instructions, future AI agents may act as co-creators, helping humans solve complex problems and make decisions. For example, in fields like healthcare, AI agents could analyze patient data and work alongside doctors to develop personalized treatment plans, continuously learning and adapting based on new information. In creative fields, AI could help artists and designers bring new ideas to life by suggesting possibilities that humans may not have considered. These agents will likely become valuable collaborators, assisting in decision-making, research, and innovation processes, rather than just performing tasks.

Another exciting possibility is the **integration of AI agents into virtual and augmented reality**. As AR and VR technologies mature, AI agents could serve as interactive guides, companions, or even co-workers in immersive environments. Imagine a future where AI agents are part of virtual meetings, offering real-time data insights, facilitating collaboration, and helping users navigate complex virtual worlds with ease. In gaming, AI agents could function as more advanced non-playable characters

(NPCs) that adapt to player behavior, creating a richer and more immersive experience.

Self-improvement will also be a hallmark of future AI agents. Operators and other advanced AI agents will likely be designed to self-optimize through feedback loops and continued learning. These systems will be able to evaluate their own performance, identify areas for improvement, and adapt in real-time, making them more efficient and effective over time. The ability to learn and adapt autonomously will not only improve task execution but also contribute to the evolution of AI agents into even more capable, intuitive, and proactive assistants.

As AI agents like Operator become increasingly sophisticated, **regulation** will become a vital aspect of their development. Governments and industry leaders will likely establish frameworks to ensure that AI evolves safely and responsibly. This will include laws and guidelines around data privacy, ethical use, and transparency, as well as how AI agents interact with humans and the wider world.

In addition to these developments, **autonomous AI systems will start to tackle challenges in industries such as space exploration, environmental sustainability, and advanced healthcare**. AI agents could assist in conducting scientific research by analyzing complex datasets, exploring new planets, managing environmental resources, and finding new medical treatments. These systems will be capable of managing large-scale, global problems, providing real-time solutions and innovative strategies.

The next generation of AI agents will be far more than just tools or assistants. They will be sophisticated, multi-dimensional systems that can understand and interact with the world in ways that were once reserved for human beings. The evolution of AI will open up a new era of productivity, creativity, and innovation, where machines not only perform tasks but also actively enhance human capabilities.

As we look to the future, it's clear that the journey of autonomous AI agents is just beginning. What started with simple, rule-based models has already evolved into dynamic, autonomous systems capable of handling complex real-world tasks. The future of AI will likely bring even more dramatic changes, pushing the boundaries of what's possible and opening up a world of new opportunities for individuals and industries alike. The potential for AI agents to revolutionize daily life, business operations, and even global challenges is immense—and we are only scratching the surface of what they can achieve.

As OpenAI continues to refine and develop Operator, the journey toward mainstream adoption is already in motion. OpenAI has been working toward a gradual rollout of this advanced AI tool, beginning with an initial release to select developers and expanding from there. The path to broad public use will likely unfold in stages, with each phase bringing its own set of challenges and opportunities for both OpenAI and the broader AI community.

Initially, the focus will be on testing Operator in controlled environments to ensure that it functions reliably and securely. During this phase, feedback from early users, particularly developers, will be crucial for identifying any technical shortcomings or areas for improvement. OpenAI has already made strides in optimizing the core functionality of the AI agent, but the true test will come as the system scales up to handle more diverse and complex tasks in real-world applications. The timeline for a full public release may depend on how quickly OpenAI can address these challenges, refine the system based on user feedback, and ensure that the technology is both stable and efficient enough for widespread use.

One of the key steps in ensuring the success of Operator's rollout will be its **integration with**

existing software and platforms. Businesses and developers need to see that implementing Operator into their workflows or applications is not only feasible but also provides real value. Operator's ability to seamlessly connect with web browsers and existing tools will play a significant role in its adoption. If developers can easily plug the AI agent into the platforms they're already using without requiring extensive rework or restructuring, the transition to AI-enhanced workflows will be smoother and more likely to gain traction.

Another crucial step in the path to widespread adoption is **education and awareness**. Many potential users may not fully understand the capabilities of autonomous AI agents like Operator or may have concerns about their implications for jobs, privacy, and security. OpenAI will need to invest in educating the public and business leaders about the benefits of AI agents and how they can transform industries and daily life. Offering clear, accessible resources, tutorials, and use cases will help demystify the technology and encourage more people to adopt it.

As Operator becomes more mainstream, ensuring its accessibility to **smaller businesses** and **individual users** will also be a key consideration. While large corporations may have the resources to implement cutting-edge AI tools, smaller companies and individuals may struggle to access the same technologies due to financial constraints or technical expertise. To address this gap, OpenAI and other AI companies may need to explore pricing models, tiered offerings, or open-source initiatives that allow more people to benefit from AI agents.

While the potential for AI to revolutionize industries and daily life is immense, the road ahead is not without its challenges. These challenges, ranging from technical limitations to ethical concerns, will need to be addressed before AI agents like Operator can reach their full potential.

One of the **technical hurdles** AI agents face is the ability to scale effectively without sacrificing performance. As AI models grow in complexity, they require more computational power and data to operate efficiently. Ensuring that AI agents like Operator can scale to handle increasingly complex tasks without overwhelming servers or running into bottlenecks is a significant concern. For businesses, this could translate into higher operational costs or slower performance if AI systems don't scale efficiently.

Another key challenge is **ensuring reliability and minimizing errors**. While probabilistic decision-making and adaptability are key strengths of AI agents, they also introduce risks. If an AI agent like Operator makes a mistake while performing a task—such as booking a flight or managing sensitive business data—the consequences could be significant. OpenAI will need to ensure that these agents are both robust and reliable, capable of handling unexpected situations without making costly errors. This will require continuous refinement of the algorithms behind AI agents and real-time monitoring systems to ensure they are functioning as expected.

In addition to technical limitations, **ethical issues** surrounding the use of autonomous AI agents will need to be addressed. One major ethical concern is how these AI agents make decisions, especially when those decisions affect individuals or businesses. Ensuring that AI agents are programmed to make ethical decisions and align with human values will be critical. OpenAI and other AI developers will need to put in place safeguards that prevent AI agents from making decisions that could harm people or society, whether through bias, discrimination, or unintentional harm.

Another ethical consideration is **accountability**. When an AI agent makes a mistake or acts in a way that has unintended consequences, who is responsible? The developers? The company using the AI? Or the AI system itself? This question of accountability will be central to discussions on the future of autonomous AI. Establishing clear guidelines for responsibility and accountability will be necessary to ensure that AI systems operate ethically and that any issues that arise are properly addressed.

From a **regulatory perspective**, the rapid advancement of autonomous AI presents significant challenges. Governments around the world will need to create frameworks for regulating AI that strike a balance between fostering innovation and ensuring safety and fairness. This will require international cooperation, as AI technology knows no borders. There will need to be clear laws governing data privacy, security, and ethical use, as well as guidelines for how AI systems should be integrated into society.

Privacy concerns will also play a major role in the development of AI agents. Autonomous systems that handle sensitive information—such as health records, financial data, and personal communications—must adhere to strict privacy standards. The risk of **data breaches**, **misuse of personal information**, or **AI agents making decisions based on biased data** could undermine public trust in AI. To mitigate these risks, OpenAI and other AI companies will need to build strong privacy protections into their systems and ensure that users have control over their data.

Despite these hurdles, the opportunities for AI to transform industries, improve efficiency, and enhance our daily lives are vast. As AI systems like Operator continue to evolve, they have the potential to create new industries, improve productivity, and drive innovation in ways we can't yet fully comprehend. The journey ahead will not be without challenges, but with careful planning, ethical considerations, and a focus on responsible development, the widespread adoption of AI agents could have a profound impact on society as a whole.

In the end, AI agents like Operator are not just about automating tasks or replacing human labor—they are about enabling humans to focus on the creative, strategic, and high-level thinking that makes us uniquely human. As this technology continues to mature, it will provide a new set of tools to solve complex problems, streamline operations, and improve quality of life for individuals and businesses alike. The future of AI is filled with promise, and the next chapter in its evolution will likely be one of the most exciting and transformative in the history of technology.

Conclusion

As we reflect on the journey of artificial intelligence, it's clear that we are at a pivotal moment in its evolution. What started as simple, rule-based systems designed to perform specific tasks has evolved into dynamic, autonomous agents capable of handling complex, real-world problems. OpenAI's Operator is the epitome of this transformation—an AI agent that doesn't just respond to commands but actively adapts, learns, and manages multi-step processes with minimal human intervention. Operator represents a bold leap forward in the capabilities of AI, one that is not just about answering questions but about becoming a true assistant, capable of tackling everything from scheduling appointments to coding software, all while learning and improving along the way.

This shift from basic chatbots to sophisticated AI agents marks the beginning of what could be the most profound technological revolution of our time. The journey from simple text-based interactions to

AI that can autonomously manage complex workflows signals a future where technology doesn't just support us—it works alongside us, taking on tasks that free up human time for more creative, strategic endeavors. But this revolution isn't just happening in the world of tech giants like OpenAI—it's already beginning to touch every industry and every aspect of our lives, from healthcare to customer service to everyday tasks like managing emails and booking flights.

As we prepare for the AI revolution, it's important to recognize that these changes are coming quickly. For businesses, the rise of autonomous AI agents like Operator presents an opportunity to dramatically increase efficiency, cut costs, and automate routine tasks, while also opening the door to new ways of interacting with customers and employees. But it's also a challenge—one that requires businesses to think critically about how they will integrate these systems into their existing workflows, how they will train their teams to work with AI, and how they will ensure that these systems are used responsibly. For individuals, the rise of AI agents offers new tools to simplify daily life, but it also requires a shift in how we approach work and the tasks we take on. We'll need to adapt, learning how to use these systems to complement our skills rather than replace them, while also being mindful of the ethical and practical challenges these systems may bring.

Looking ahead, the vision for a smarter, more efficient world powered by AI agents is both exciting and inspiring. As these technologies continue to develop, we will see them become even more integrated into our lives, tackling more complex problems and enabling us to achieve things that once seemed impossible. From industries like healthcare, where AI can help doctors make better decisions, to business operations that rely on automation to streamline processes, the potential is limitless. And while the road ahead is not without challenges—technical limitations, ethical dilemmas, and regulatory hurdles—it's clear that AI is poised to reshape the way we live, work, and interact with the world around us.

The future of AI is not a distant, abstract concept—it's happening now. The tools and agents we've seen evolve, like Operator, are just the beginning. In the years to come, AI will continue to evolve, becoming more intuitive, more integrated, and more capable of handling the complexities of the world we live in. As this transformation takes place, we must embrace it, adapt to it, and guide its development in ways that ensure it serves humanity's best interests. With the right approach, we can create a future where AI is not just a tool, but a trusted partner—one that helps us navigate the challenges of tomorrow and unlocks the vast potential of the future.

We stand at the threshold of a smarter world—one where autonomous AI agents like Operator are the norm, not the exception. As we continue on this journey, the possibilities are endless, and the future of AI promises to be a transformative force in shaping the world to come.

www.ingramcontent.com/pod-product-compliance
Lightning Source LLC
Chambersburg PA
CBHW071028240526
45469CB00006BD/2131